D0273478

How to Train Your Dog

CONTENTS

Dedication
To Mum and Dad for all your love and support.
To Simon and the gang - for always being there.

Photographs by Frank Naylor with the kind co-operation of members of Petersfield & District Dog Training Club. Special thanks to Karen Thackray.

KINGDOM

©2001 by Kingdom Books PO9 5TT ENGLAND

Hi, welcome to class! In this book I will try to explain how to teach your dog the basic commands that will make life simple and pleasant for both of you. A well trained dog is a joy to own and is something that can be achieved with just a little planning and practice.

First of all, why bother to train dogs? Why not just add them to the family without having to invest time and effort in training them? Well, we all know dogs who never seem to leave the house, who are shut away when visitors call, who are kept in the back garden, or who are never allowed off the lead in the park. Why? The most likely answer is that the dog will not obey the owner. Perhaps the dog will not come when he is called (a very common problem), maybe he is boisterous or anti-social towards other dogs, jumps up at people, will eat whatever he can find, and so on. It must be admitted that there are also, sadly, some owners who have no intention of providing their dogs with even the basic requirements - good food, regular exercise, grooming, training and, of course, attention. This is a big pity because they are missing out on so much. Lazy owners dismiss their dogs as being 'disobedient' or, worse still, consider it quite normal to shut a dog away because they have not taught him how to

With a little guidance all dogs can be taught how to behave.

SOCIALISATION

behave. Dogs are not mind readers and they are not machines. They cannot be expected to know what we want unless they are first shown and then given the chance to learn through repetition and reward.

The good news is that most dogs *can* be trained to follow basic commands which will make your life much easier. The simple truth is that dogs want a pack leader - they need someone to be in charge and, fortunately for us, most love to learn things and show off what they know. Like children, dogs are much happier when they know what the limits are and who to refer to when they are unhappy or in need. If he doesn't have this, the dog will do his own thing but, believe me, he will be much happier if *you* set the guidelines. You will get far more out of the relationship if you can teach your dog to do the following things:

- Be sociable with other dogs and people

- Come when called (recall)

- Sit

- Down

- Stay

- Retrieve

I will show you how to teach these things to either a puppy or an adult, and also what to do if you have an older dog with problems.....

(Throughout the book I use one of my dog's names - 'Mikki' - to illustrate a command; just swop your dog's name for his!)

Socialisation

I am a firm believer in getting a puppy out and about when he is young so that he can take in the sights and sounds of the world at an age when most things are easily accepted. I appreciate that the young dog will not yet be fully covered by his vaccinations so I try to minimise the risk by carrying the pup where appropriate (so that he cannot sniff places where other dogs might have been) and I only introduce him to dogs who are vaccinated. The following are places I like to take a puppy:

- Dog training clubs
- Schools
- Railway stations (and on public transport, if relevant)
- Shopping precincts and garden centres
- Car parks

In these situations the pup will meet other dogs, children and adults of both sexes and a variety of ages. He will also see traffic and hear loud sounds. You might think "We don't have any children, so why should I socialise him with them?" or, "I live on my own, so he doesn't need to meet the opposite sex." Big mistake! It is precisely for this reason that he needs to be introduced to them. Make a point of letting your pup meet both children and adults, male and female, of all ages. Remember though, it is your job to protect him from any unpleasant or overbearing characters. Put yourself in the dog's shoes and don't let him be overwhelmed. If someone is being pushy (and most people can't resist pups), I say "I'm just letting him get his bearings" and they usually get the message and back off. If another dog is being rough with my youngster I would push him away and ask the owner to call him off. If this doesn't work, pick the pup up and walk away.

If you have a shy dog do not let people force themselves on him - this will only make him more panicky. Instead, ask them to ignore him and not to give him eye contact. I would carry a tub of cubed cheese or sausage for this purpose; strangers may offer him a titbit, without looking at him, but they are then to ignore him again. Your dog should be allowed to approach them in his own time, if and when he is ready to do so.

The shy dog can be taught to become more confident through the use of play at home (see *Retrieve*), through teaching him tricks and by taking him around with you as much as possible - initially, just to look and observe. We recently took on Jemma, a gorgeous four and a half month old pup who was completely unsocialised. When we first got her, although happy and confident at home, she was scared of people, other dogs, traffic and loud noises - to the extent that she wanted to run home if anything spooked her. The photos opposite catalogue our progress, as described below.

I began by walking Jem in quiet areas (virtually no traffic or people). I also put her on an extending lead so that she could explore and forge ahead in safe surroundings, which helped to increase her confidence. This was gradually built up until she would accept titbits off strangers and could start to be walked through shopping precincts, garden centres, around housing estates and so on. To get her used to other dogs I took her to dog training clubs where we would sit at the back of the hall so that she could watch them but feel safe. Once she was coping with this, I then added puppy training classes, which meant meeting dogs at closer quarters and learning to obey basic commands with them around. Jemma has made an amazing amount of progress over the 7 weeks we have had her. Patience and perseverance have been the keywords. However, all this could have been avoided with early socialisation.

If, on the other hand, your pup loves everyone and everything, you will need to impress upon him that not everyone wants to be leapt upon. Teach him to sit before being patted or when being greeted. If he learns to keep all four feet on the ground, he will be much more acceptable to other people. We own a young male who is very friendly and loves to jump up at people to say hello,

Early socialisation is vital. If you have a shy dog, take things slowly.

THE EARLY DAYS

The correct way to greet someone!

but a dog bouncing around at head height can be frightening, especially to children and elderly folk. Raising a knee or gently squeezing his front paws will dissuade your dog from doing this and you can then ask him to sit instead for his reward.

Over-friendly dogs may also find it more difficult to concentrate - and therefore to obey you - when other dogs and people are around, because they are dying to go over and say hello. So it is vital that you and your rewards are more interesting than the distractions, and also that you can enforce the 'come' command.

We will discuss how to achieve this in the *Recall* section. These dogs would also benefit from attending training classes (as would *all* dogs), to put them in a situation where they are surrounded by other dogs but learn to pay attention to their owner.

The Early Days

Before we get onto the subject of training per se, I would like to discuss how a puppy or young dog is introduced into our household and his early training begun.

Housetraining is part of the initial early training and is another hurdle which can make or break a dog's relationship with his humans. If you are getting a puppy, do yourself a big favour and buy a crate (indoor kennel) before you bring the pup home. These can be purchased quite reasonably, either secondhand or new, and will last indefinitely. They can be made nice and cosy for the pup by adding vet bed, a soft old jumper, a small teddy bear (remove any detachable parts first) and a water bowl. I also drape a blanket over the sides to make it more cave-like. We have a crate in the lounge and bedroom, until the pup is past his housetraining and teething stage. (If you do not wish to buy one, someone at your local dog training club might be willing to lend you one.) By the way, for safety reasons, never ever leave a puppy's collar on when he is in the crate.

On his first day in your new home, carry your pup to the crate and let him see you throw in a few really tasty

Mealtimes are an ideal way of introducing a puppy to his crate.

titbits. He will probably want to go in and eat them (if not, use something even more appetising). Praise him while he is in there and allow him to come out straight away if he wants. Next, make up the pup's meal and pop it and the pup in the crate, still leaving the door open. Again, allow the pup to come out when he wants. Then, when you can see that he is getting tired, gently carry him to the crate and shut him in. Stay in the room but try to ignore him. If he starts to whine, leave the room and wait until he is quiet before going back and releasing him. If he sleeps, great. When he wakes, pick him up and carry him straight out to the garden so that he can be clean. I say "Go bizzies" and quietly praise the pup while he is doing his business.

It is important to stay with the pup while he is in the garden - that way you will know he has been and it will also give him confidence (remember, everything is new and strange to him in the beginning). If he doesn't need to go, I will keep an eye on him and leave the back door open anyway so that he has the chance to go out; I will then take him back out again ten or fifteen minutes later. If you keep taking the pup outside, he will get the idea that this is where he performs, particularly once he has 'been' a couple of times and his scent is laid down.

The following are signs that a pup needs to go - he may put his nose to the floor, have an earnest look on his face, circle, break into a run and so on. There are also certain times when he will need to empty - first thing in the morning, after meals, after playing, last thing at night. Although it is said that pups need to go every two hours, I find that if they are running around (under your supervision, of course), they need to go more often in the first few months. Having other adult dogs around is also a help because your pup will see them going out to be clean and, being a pack animal, won't want to be left behind. In the beginning take care that the other adults don't distract the pup from the job in hand by wanting to play with him. Life's a balancing act!

Having already spent some time in the crate during his first day, you are now ready to tackle the sleeping arrangements! Incidentally, I also make a point of going round to see the neighbours first, to explain that we have a new pup who might be a bit noisy to start with, while he gets used to the crate.

It is up to you where your dog sleeps at night. Ours sleep upstairs with us. There are a couple of reasons for this:

- We really love their company.
- You get to see all their behaviours, including playing last thing at night and first thing in the morning, which you would otherwise miss.
- I hate the thought that if my dog was ill and needed me in the middle of the night, I wouldn't know about it until it was possibly too late.
- Finally, as we both work, I feel every moment we spend with the dogs is precious.

As mentioned previously, we have an upstairs and downstairs crate. When its time for bed, the dogs go into the garden for one last wee and then its upstairs for a goodnight biscuit and lights out. The pup goes into his crate with a few extra biscuits to occupy him whilst I close the door. I would not expect a young pup (under the age of 4-5 months, say) to last through the night, so be prepared to get up and take him out him when he cries to let you know its time! This will involve broken sleep until the pup is a little bit older but it is worth it because you will not have a howling, distressed puppy in the kitchen overnight and a dirty floor awaiting you in the morning. Crating the pup overnight will also encourage him to keep his area clean, which will help in the housetraining process. Carry the pup out to the garden the moment he is released from the crate - he may not be able to hang on while you sleepily search for shoes and trousers, so have a dressing gown and slippers handy. The pup will probably want to urinate and defecate first thing in the morning, so make sure he does both before you come back in again. By around 5 months of age my pup is usually sleeping happily on the bed through the night and then its just a case of going downstairs to put him out as soon as he wakes.

The routine during the day will vary according to your own particular schedule but, of course, the pup will need plenty of opportunities to be clean. If you are at home all day so much the better, because you will be able to spend time with and watch the pup, allow him access to the garden, and praise him for getting it right. If he makes a mistake, do not scold him. The fault was yours for not taking him out in time. If you lose your temper and make an issue of housetraining you will only prolong the process and make it harder for all concerned. Clean up the mistake and resolve to get there sooner next time.

If you cannot be there all the time, I consider an hour or two to be the very maximum I would leave a young puppy crated before he needed to have his next meal, human company and to use the garden again. He only has a small bladder so cannot be expected to hold on for very long. (An indoor pen will give the growing pup more space while you are out but he is less likely to be clean and may develop some horrible habits if his faeces are left lying around too long.)

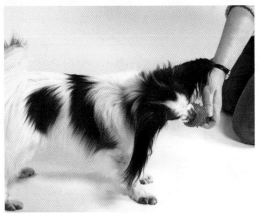

In addition to the usual crate contents, a couple of stuffed Rhinos or Nylabones will also help to keep him occupied and soften your absence. Rhinos (which can also be used as throw toys) are excellent because their hollow centres can be filled

Dogs love stuffed Rhinos.

with scraps, dog biscuits, bits of cheese or sausage and sealed with a cheese spread or meat paste. Their hardwearing nature means that they are also good for teething pups.

If they have to be left, our older pups are crated for a couple of hours maximum until they are housetrained and no longer teething. The crate is in the lounge, there are a couple of adult dogs around and the radio and lights are left on for their comfort. My neighbours have also, in the past, popped in and stayed with a pup when he was young, letting him out for a wee and keeping him company for a while. If you have friends, family or neighbours who will help out, this is ideal for the working owner. (For older dogs that can be trusted, a dog flap may also be useful so the dog has access to a secure garden when you are out.)

Once the youngster is older (6-7 months), I would begin leaving him in the lounge or kitchen for a short period of time, with a sensible adult dog for

Just helping myself to a Nylabone....

As no batteries were available on this occasion, Marvie settled for crisps.

company if possible. Make sure he has been well exercised (a training session will also tire him out mentally) and has plenty of safe toys/chews to occupy him or he may find his own amusement! Remove all valuables and chewables, and use a babygate across the door so he can still see out. Build this up and, if he is clean and does not chew anything, extend this freedom until he has the run of the house, or as much room as you wish to give him. If he is destructive (and this is not due to teething), you will have to rethink this.

Firstly, you will need to decide whether your dog has separation anxiety or is chewing for the sheer sake of it before deciding how to tackle the problem. We have a young dog (eleven months old) who will chew candles, batteries, pens, tapes, dried flowers, plastic bottles, in fact anything he can get his paws on. He has even done it under our noses - exploring worktops and peeling wallpaper while we were in the same room! This is not caused by separation anxiety because (a) he has done it in our presence and (b) he is a very confident, independent dog. If you have a destructive dog and don't wish to crate him or restrict him to a chewproof area, try popping back unexpectedly, especially in the first few minutes after you have left him - if he thinks you could reappear at any time he is less likely to look for mischief. You could also set traps for him on the surfaces where he likes to poach, so he gets a surprise when he is being naughty. Coating items with bitter apple spray, mustard or hot sauce can also be a deterrent. This type of dog probably needs more to occupy his

EXERCISE

The joys of free running.

mind so, in addition to his obedience classes, Marvie will be starting Agility shortly. He is also insured, like the rest of our dogs.

Separation anxiety is too big a topic to cover in this book but I would make a start by encouraging the dog to be a bit more independent so he can cope better on his own. This might include making him spend time in another room several times a day, crating him for very short periods of time and giving him attention on your terms, not his.

Exercise

Exercise is vital for *all* dogs. Not only does it allow him to vent pent-up energy and frustration but it is important for the dog to get away from the four walls that surround him most of the time. For many, a trip to the local park is a social occasion when the dogs from the neighbourhood get to sniff each other and examine the latest lamp-post gossip. I have to confess that our dogs are not the slightest bit interested in any of that. They have only one aim in mind when they are out - to run their hearts out. Collies will run until they drop and, five

13

minutes after returning from a walk, will be ready to go all over again. They also need considerable mental stimulation. Our dogs spend half an hour flat out chasing frisbees in the morning (the youngsters are roadwalked separately until they are around 6-7 months old), with an even longer session in the evening. In addition, they usually receive some sort of training during the day, attend obedience clubs several nights a week and compete at the weekend.

There are 2 reasons why the youngsters are roadwalked separately:

1. It is a continuation of their socialisation, because they will see children, traffic, neighbours, the postman, milkman and other dogs on their walk.

2. This one-to-one time is used to get the pup into me so that he looks to me for his fun and for instruction. Collies are pack animals and, combined with the herding instinct, a pup who is allowed to run free with the adults invariably ends up chasing them and trying to nip them or hang off their ears. This is unfair on the other dogs so it is best not to let it start in the first place. (Regardless of breed, it is important to socialise your new puppy separately from your other adult dogs so that he learns to be confident in his own right.)

Exercise takes many forms - it could mean a run on the beach, in fields, swimming, chasing frisbees, walking through the woods, on the hills, along a country footpath, and so on. In addition to throwing frisbees (which ours chase as they land and roll along the ground), we also go for long walks to remind them that they are dogs. Even then they will jump up and insist on having a toy, so often I relent and let them carry a tennis ball. There is nothing nicer than seeing a pack interact on a walk and, for me, it is one of the joys of ownership. (By the way, don't forget your 'poo bags' when you are out.)

Recall

Having discussed how to settle your pup into his new home and establish a routine, we can move onto training the basics. The very first thing I want my pup to learn is to run to me as soon as I call his name. If he will not come when he is called, I cannot let him off the lead in the park or fields - in fact he cannot be loose anywhere except in a house or garden. Therefore he won't be able to enjoy off-lead exercise and so his outings won't be much fun. Extending leads are all very well but you can't beat a good gallop and the satisfaction of seeing your dog bouncing around and returning happily whenever you call him. This is easily achieved, without the pup or adult dog even realising you are training him.

You can use mealtimes to begin the process - make up the dog's meal and then call his name in a happy voice ("Mikki, come!"). When he arrives, give him lots of praise and put his food down for him. Next time, have some cheese or a piece of tasty sausage and call the dog to you again. Bend down and make a

Recall training can start with the first meal.

real fuss of him. This is a happy time! You want the dog to anticipate that if you call his name it will lead to something nice, so the sooner he gets there the better. Initially, try not to use his name if you have to tell him off for something. His name should have a pleasant association. Practise these fun recalls in the house and garden.

Getting the dog to sit straight in front of you is referred to as 'the present'. I don't often ask the dog to present at the end of a recall because this can slow up his response - it is more important for the dog to respond quickly and happily than to have to think about whether he is sitting straight or not. If you start to correct the dog for the sit, you may ignore the fact that he has done the hardest part of the exercise, which is to return to you.

When you get a positive response every time, it is time to try somewhere different. Choose a quiet place with little to distract your dog. Let him go off and explore, then call him in the same happy tone as before. As you do so, walk

15

away briskly, which should encourage your dog to quickly rejoin you. As soon as he reaches you, give him his titbit and make a fuss of him. **Then let him go again, as his reward.** If he is a little more independent, run and hide behind a

It is vital that the dog is released again after the recall.

tree or building, so he learns that if he doesn't respond quickly he will get left behind.

If he still ignores you, attach a long line (for example, a washing-line) to his collar so you can reinforce the command. Even if you are making him obey, still encourage the dog and walk or run away from him, giving the dog his toy or titbit when he reaches you. Then let him go again. You might feel daft running away from your dog but it will encourage a sense of urgency.

The release is vital - otherwise dogs quickly learn that once their owner calls them, the walk is over. If that was the case, would you feel like obeying?!

If you have a dog with recall problems or who is easily distracted, use the long line, a tub of cubed cheese/sausage or your dog's favourite toy so you can have a game with him, and train the recalls in an enclosed space such as a tennis court or yard so that you can control the situation. Once your dog learns that you can insist upon obedience, because you can back-up what you say, he will learn that it is easier to give in. But you must persevere, even if it means taking half an hour to catch the dog and then letting him go again! Never tell the dog off after he has come to you - tempting though this may be - or you will shatter any trust he has in you. Grit your teeth, praise, reward, and release him again. (If you need to tell him off, it would be

Using the long line to back up the recall command. The handler also uses a titbit to encourage her dog.

Ready to recall with another dog present.

better to go over and catch him in the act; then get the dog to do something easy, such as 'sit', so that you can praise him.)

Once the dog will obey with no distractions, I would then ask a friend to use their dog as a decoy. We would go to the same place, release our dogs and allow them to play. I would then call my dog and, if he didn't respond on the first command, I would use the long line to reel him in, reward and release. Repeat until the dog shows sign of coming to you without the tug on the line, then praise like mad and quit while you are ahead - you will be sowing good seeds in your dog's mind.

The long line is also very useful for reinforcing commands such as 'wait' and the instant down. If your dogs bully each other when running free, the long line can also be used to stop the bully in his tracks (say 'Mikki leave!' before you step on it or pick it up, to give the dog fair warning and so that he learns what the command means). Although dogs may be quite obedient at home, to begin with they may not be quite so responsive in other situations, so the long line is a gentle reminder that you are still in charge and expect them to listen to you, regardless of what is going on around them.

Marvie, our young farm-bred collie, was a real challenge to train. The other dogs are very good when I call them but Marvie would just stand and stare and then refuse to get back into the car at the end of a run. I tried everything - food and toys (not interested, his freedom was more important), driving off (this usually worked but wasn't always practical), walking in the opposite direction (he didn't care, or would follow at a distance), and so on. The annoying thing was that if he saw a dog or person, he would run off to say hello to them. As he also likes to jump up, this wasn't always welcome. And even if the other person didn't mind, I did.

Teaching the 'wait' at a distance, using the long line, could be a life saver.

Finally I decided to use a long line, for the first time ever. It worked because Marvie realised that not only did I mean what I said but, more importantly, I could now enforce it. (He was also castrated as we do not plan to breed from him.) His recall and instant down are now reliable but, in hindsight, I would use a long line much earlier if the dog showed signs of doing his own thing instead of listening to me. Happily, you will find that once your dog starts to obey, it becomes habit and you set up a successful cycle (as opposed to a vicious circle!) Incidentally, it is important to praise your dog for all the good things he does - don't just speak to him when you want to tell him off or pretty soon he'll stop listening altogether.

Sit

The sit is an easy command to teach but the way in which it is taught has changed, for the better, over the last few years. Previously, owners were taught

Luring Jem into the sit.

to manhandle the dog into position - using their hand to push down on their dog's rear end, saying 'Sit" at the same time. Not surprisingly, some dogs resisted this but were just pushed about more as a result, turning it into a wrestling match! Here's the new, kinder way of teaching it:

- Have your dog in a quiet part of the house, along with some cheese or titbits

- Stand or kneel beside your dog (he should be standing)

- Use a piece of cheese to get his attention

- Slowly move the cheese towards his nose and then up and backwards over his head (it should pass between his ears). As you do so, say "Mikki, sit". Tip: do not lift the cheese too high or the dog will jump up for it

- As your dog follows the movement of the cheese, his head will rise and, as a result, his bottom will lower to the floor. Mission accomplished!

- Give the dog his reward whilst he is still sitting and, at the same time, press his bottom gently on the floor to reinforce what he is doing and say "Good sit"

- It is useful to have a release word for all the exercises, so the dog knows when he can break off. I say "Okay".

Down

The down follows on naturally from the sit and can be taught when the dog is either standing or sitting (from the sit is easier because the body is already partially lowered, you just need to get the front half down!)

- Again, work in a quiet place, armed with some cheese or titbits

- Kneel down beside your dog (it is easier if you are at his level)

- Use a piece of cheese to get his attention

- Have the cheese between your fingers so the dog cannot get it. Then, still holding the cheese, place it on the floor just in front of the dog, between his front paws.

- As your dog tries to get the cheese, his head will drop and, if you are lucky, his shoulders will follow, his front legs will buckle and his body will lower to

Clockwise (starting with main picture): (1). Reinforcing the sit by gently pressing Jem's
bottom on the floor. (2). Luring Jem into the down - note the position of the titbit.
(3). Reinforcing the down and rewarding the dog whilst she is still in position.

the floor. However, if you have the cheese too close to the dog's body, he
won't be able to do this because your hand will be in the way. On the other
hand, if you hold the cheese too far in front of him, he will simply get up
and walk to it, not knowing what you want. So it is important to hold the
cheese in the right place relative to the dog. If the dog is standing and
lowers his front half but not his back end, a little gentle pressure on the rear
end should be enough to get his bottom on the floor.

- As he assumes the position, say "Mikki, down". I use a deeper tone of voice
  than for the Sit, to help the dog differentiate.

Quietly reassuring Mikki in the first stage of the Down Stay.

Handler is now upright but remains beside the dog. A hand signal is also helpful.

Starting to move further away, handler stands sideways on to the dog.

- Give the dog his reward whilst he is in the down and, at the same time, press his bottom gently on the floor to reinforce what he is doing and say "Good down".

- Use your release word and have a game.

It is up to you how quickly you want your dog to respond. You can speed him up by applying gentle pressure between his shoulder blades as he goes down. Doing this a couple of times, with plenty of praise, will convince him that you mean 'now!' It is quite useful to do this with a puppy anyway, to get them into the habit of being quick. If your dog knows the command but takes his time, he might be subtly challenging your authority. This is something to consider if you are having problems in other areas, such as not coming back when called, reluctance to give up his toys, and ignoring other commands.

Dominant dogs may initially be reluctant to obey the down command, because it is a submissive position but, if they are rewarded with a tasty titbit and a game afterwards, they will realise that it is an easy way of getting something nice out of you! This method is particularly suitable for dominant dogs and big breeds because there is no confrontation and no pushing and shoving involved.

If you have been taught to scoop your dog's front legs from underneath him, or to lift one front leg and push down on the shoulder blades to get him into the down, all well and good if this method works for you. If not, or if your dog is slow, try the above method.

Stay

You can choose either the sit or down position when teaching the dog to stay (in competition you will need to learn both, as well as a stand stay in the higher classes). It does not matter which one you choose, but the down is probably a more stable and comfortable position for the dog. The important thing when teaching a dog to stay is to make progress slowly. Stays are all about confidence and, if you are in too much of a hurry to make distance or get out of sight, you will end up rushing the process, to the dog's detriment. This is how I teach a dog to stay down:

- Have your dog on a collar and lead in a quiet place.

- Lure your dog into the down, using a titbit, and praise him quietly.

- Tell your dog that he is going to do a Down Stay. Keep the lead loose and just kneel beside him, stroking him gently. Say "That's a good Down Stay".

- Be ready to gently but quickly push your dog back into the down, by applying pressure on the shoulder blades, if he should move. You should be

Mikki and Misty have been taught to lie flat in competition, making it harder for them to break the stay.

watching him like a hawk because all this is new to him and he may decide at any moment that he has lost interest or doesn't like it.

- Keep talking soothingly to your dog, to keep his attention, and count to three in your head. Then praise your dog while he is still lying down, release him and have a game. (Be careful if you use titbits to teach the stay because the dog may be tempted to break to get to the food.) Tip: do not use the dog's name during the stay or he may get up and come to you, thinking that you have called him.

- Once your dog accepts the down and will lie quietly watching you, extend the time to five seconds, then ten and so on, up to one minute. Next, try standing up but, again, be ready to correct the dog if he tries to move. A hand signal is also useful to reinforce the stay. I hold my right hand up, palm facing the dog, to indicate that I do not want him to move.

- If the dog stays while you are standing beside him, move half a step away but keep watching him and be ready to correct at any moment. You should still be talking to your dog, telling him what a clever down he is doing. If he is allowed to switch off or look away, he will probably forget what he is doing and either start sniffing around or get up and walk off! As you return to your dog, say "Down, good down" again, in a low voice, because he may be so pleased that you are back, that he breaks to greet you. Make him wait a second or so before you release him, so that he does not start getting up in anticipation of being released.

- The next stage is to move a full pace away, then two, then three. If you face your dog he may think it is a Recall, so stand sideways on instead. It is also very important to use the command "Stay" not "Wait". "Stay" means remain where you are, I will be coming back to release you. "Wait" means I will be calling you shortly and you will get up and come to me.

- If your dog is steady, try walking round him whilst he is in the down. Then clap, or bend down and pretend to pick something up off the floor. All these things will test your dog and you will see if he understands what you have taught him so far. If the dog breaks at any time, don't get cross with him. Simply pick up his lead, say "Don't cheat!" in a lighthearted voice and put him back in the same place. Only this time, go back a stage or two to remind him what you want.

- Once you are ready to start going out of sight, choose somewhere you can still watch the dog. I use the lounge because after I walk out of the lounge into the hall, I can look through the crack of the door. I am literally only out of sight for a second - during which time I will be looking through the gap to see what the dog's reaction is - and then I appear again. I praise the dog for staying ("Good stay") whilst I am standing in the doorway and then I disappear again, for another second or two. I then return to the dog, talking to him and praising him quietly all the time. Stand by his side for a couple of seconds before praising, releasing and having a game.

- If you want to know if your dog really understands what he is doing, try using the lead to gently pull him out of the down. He should resist you. Do not try this until the dog is experienced or you will undo all your good work!

The down stay can be adapted for all kinds of situations. In domestic situations, I say "Stop there" which means remain there until I release you. This could be when we are in someone else's home, outside the shops, in the park, out on a walk, and so on. "Stop there" means that although the dog has to stay in position, I don't expect him to lie stock still. I am not asking for the rigid position holding which I would expect in the stay ring at a show. There is no confusion because (a) the two situations are completely different and (b) my dogs are taught to lie flat on their sides in the competitive down stay, which should make it more difficult for them to break position in the stay ring.

Retrieve

The Retrieve will be easier to teach your dog if he likes to play and, conversely, if he likes to play, he will probably enjoy the Retrieve more. Aside from the Recall, one of the first things I do with my new pup is to see how strong his play is. To do this I get a soft ragger or tuggy ball and secure a lead round it so that the toy can be dragged along the floor or whizzed up in the air, all at arm's length from me.

- The tuggy is a good toy to use because (a) it is soft in the dog's mouth and (b) it is big enough for him to be able to grab it and hold it easily.

- The lead allows me to be part of the game and to control it without being too dominating in the early stages when you want the dog to gain strength and confidence. I find that if you use something like a tennis ball or a

25

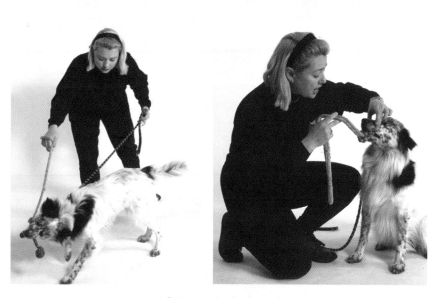

Left: Encouraging the dog to play.
Right: Teaching the give, using fingers over the top of the mouth.

squeaky toy, it is hard to share it with the pup and you will be tempted to take it away from him so that you can throw it.

To start, I have the pup alone in the lounge, show him the toy and then drag it quickly along the floor, away from him. This seems to awaken the chase instinct in most dogs because they usually pounce on it straight away. If so, great because now we can play tuggies. If not, I will egg the dog on whilst making sure that I am just a bit quicker with the lead than the dog is with his feet, to keep the toy just out of reach. If he cannot catch the toy, this will usually make him frustrated and more eager to get it. It is important that the toy moves away from the dog, to make it a challenge. If you wave it under his nose or in his face he will not be interested because this is not very stimulating. Your voice is also crucial - if you sound excited and hypey, the dog will pick up on this and get excited too. You have to convince the dog that he wants to play and that if he is not quick enough he won't be able to catch it. Only whisk the toy away a few times then make sure the dog gets it, otherwise he may lose interest.

Once the dog has got the toy in his mouth, do not pull too hard on the lead. If you rip it out of his mouth, you may hurt him and put him off. Let him get a good grip and then use the lead to play tuggies with it. You can twist the dog in a little circle, run up and down with him, or just wiggle the lead from side to side. All the time you should be egging your dog on and praising him for playing.

The next important thing is to teach the dog to give the toy up. Some will do this straight away as soon as you say their name and the command "Give" in a firm voice. Others may need a finger and thumb inserted either side of their mouth to open it up for the toy to be released. If you hear any growling, immediately tell the pup off and take the toy away sternly. Then allow the pup to have the toy again and then say "Give" again. If the pup gives the toy up, make a big fuss of him and let him have the toy. If not, open his mouth and take it away again, being ready to correct again if he growls. It is really important to be able to take anything off your dog at anytime, and he must realise this. Although a small pup growling may seem cute, comical or threatening - depending on the dog and your point of view - it is the slippery slope to the dog being dominant over you and should be nipped in the bud immediately. If you leave it, telling yourself that it is not important or that you'll sort it out another day, you will soon be faced with a dog who is no longer a pup and who can do you real harm with his teeth, if he wants to.

Incidentally, some say that you should not play tuggy games with your dog or allow him free access to toys. We play these games with all our dogs and they have two overflowing toy boxes - one in the bedroom and one in the lounge. These are full of tennis balls, raggies, cardboard tubes, taped up magazines, teddies, soft toys, tuggy balls, empty pop bottles, cows' hooves and so on. If we are busy the dogs amuse themselves by chewing on their toys or chasing each

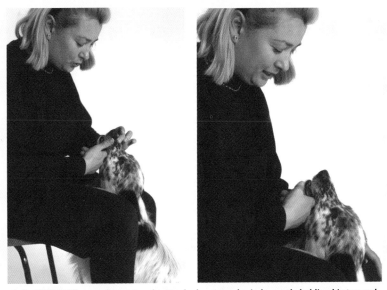

Left: Mikki holding my finger; I make sure he has a good grip by gently holding his top and bottom jaw. Right: Holding the finger without help.

other round with them. Why should we deprive them of this pleasure? They never argue over toys (there are plenty to choose from and there are no dominance issues in the pack, they all know where they fit in) and visiting dogs are welcome to join in. Playing tuggy games and leaving toys around is not an issue unless you have control problems in other areas of your relationship (for example, if your dog is possessive or guards things). As long as the dog will give the toy up when you say so, no problem.

Now that we have the dog holding and giving, I will put the retrieve in a slightly more formal context. The stages are:

1. Firstly, I teach the dog to hold my finger. Have the dog sitting in front of you. Aim your right hand index finger gently into the left side of his mouth and pop it in. Use your left hand to gently hold the dog's jaws together (to stop him spitting the finger out, as he will try to do in the early stages). Be gentle when you hold his jaws or you will panic him. Also, do not block his nostrils or eyes! Hold your finger in his mouth for only a second, whilst you say "Mikki hold", praise him and then say "Give" and remove it.

    The reason I use a finger to start with is that I can tell from this how well the dog is gripping and, therefore, whether he needs to get exert more pressure. (If you are at all worried about this, go to the next stage instead.) Keep doing this until you can see that the dog is actually opening his mouth in anticipation of the finger going in.

Holding a taped-up magazine, with and then without help.

2. Find a simple article, such as a small, taped-up magazine. Sit on the edge of a chair with the dog in front of you. Say "Mikki hold" and use your left hand to open his mouth whilst the right one pops the article in. Gently hold both jaws shut whilst you quietly praise. Count to two, release your grip and say "Give" at the same time. (Tip: massaging the back of the dog's head with your right hand will help him to relax and accept the hold.)

3. Build this up until the dog will open his mouth as the article approaches. Then you can hold the article in his mouth for a little longer but continue to supervise the hold by gently holding his muzzle. If the dog turns his head away, gently push it back and proceed as normal.
   The important thing is to persevere because once your dog realises you mean business, he will start to co-operate. You can use titbits to reward but the dog may spit the article out in anticipation of getting the sweet! If you are having problems, ask yourself if the article is suitable or whether you are doing something to put him off - such as banging his teeth, blocking his nostrils or eyes, or using the wrong tone of voice (either too harsh or too soft). Patience and timing are also crucial; most people let go of the muzzle too soon or leave the article in for too long. Do not test the dog at this stage!

4. Once the dog is holding confidently, I will start to allow him to hold it by

Left: Holding the article in the present. My hands are ready to correct if necessary.
Right: Moving forward to take the article.

Top left: Holding article (to encourage the dog) on the floor .
Top right: Backing off and asking the dog to present.
Main picture: Using an extending lead to guarantee the return from a distance.

himself, initially by removing pressure on the upper jaw. I then stand in front of the dog and ask him to hold the article in the present position. I will stroke his head gently so that my hands are there in case he goes to open his mouth too soon - I am then ready to correct him and prevent him dropping the article. Don't forget to quietly praise your dog while he is holding ("Good hold, that's a clever boy, well done").

5. Next, I have the dog sitting or standing beside me and I hold the article just out of reach so that he has to lean forward to get it. I then back off and guide him into the present. If he can do this, I will move on to holding the article a foot or two away and then start lowering it gradually to the floor so that he has to get up, walk a pace or two and reach down to get the article.

6. The ultimate step is to place the article on the floor, still holding it with your right hand to give the dog confidence. When your dog has picked it up, guide him into the present position and - hey presto! you have a retrieve.

To encourage the dogs to enjoy retrieving, ours are given all kinds of things to hold and play with as youngsters, including cardboard inner tubes, empty cartons, flowerpots, boxes, packaging, plastic tubing, carpet pieces and so on.
Once the hold is established, I will put the dog on an extending lead, throw the toy a short way and let the dog dash after it. As soon as he has picked it up, I will kneel down and call the dog to me, using the lead to encourage him back if necessary. If the dog is a bit iffy about picking it up, race him out there and kick the toy or grab it yourself. Laugh and tease him by holding the toy into you and wheel away from him, so that he really wants it. The next time you throw it, if he is quicker, allow him to pick it up himself and praise him thoroughly. Then leave it for that session and have a rethink. Perhaps your dog needs an article which he is keener on? Maybe you inhibited him a bit in the early stages and he needs a bit of egging on and permission to be bolder.
If your dog is reluctant to bring the toy back, practise on an extending lead in an enclosed area (eg the kitchen). Have another toy on you to 'swop' for his and don't always take the toy off him - this will make him more willing to return.
The retrieve can be used to exercise your dog (ours are individually taught to fetch a frisbee before they are allowed to run with the gang), to play games such as seeking a hidden article, or to fulfil a purpose such as finding lost keys. I also use my dogs' love of toys to teach competition exercises such as heelwork, sendaways and distance control.
99% of my training is done through play - I only use food when teaching puppies the recall, sit and down. Play gives a dog spring in his step and a real zest for learning.

Training Clubs

Training clubs range from large Championship show clubs to small un-registered

Jem learning to ignore the other dogs at club, with the aid of a tasty titbit.

ones. Details of your local clubs can be obtained from The Kennel Club, from Dog Training Weekly (see Useful Addresses for both), veterinary clinics, pet shops or word of mouth from other dog owners in your area. Instructors should use only kind methods - the days of check chains and compulsion are long gone. You will have to judge for yourself whether or not a club has moved with the times - leave your dog at home for the first visit and use your eyes and ears. Are the dogs happy and willing? Are the trainers able to adapt to the different breeds? Can they offer solutions when things are not going to plan? A good trainer will keep the class on its toes, be able to spot and correct faults and, if necessary, be able to demonstrate what she means.

Be respectful to the trainer, explain what you are hoping to achieve and most will be more than happy to help. If something is not covered in a class which you particularly wish to learn or practise, do say so as trainers welcome ideas and feedback from class members. Conversely, if something will not suit you or your dog, explain this to the trainer and ask to sit this one out.

You will need your tastiest treats and the dog's favourite toys for club nights. If your dog is overwhelmed initially by the surroundings, ask to sit at the back until the dog is relaxed (this may take several sessions, so be patient). Then get him to do something simple that he knows, such as 'sit', or even just playing, so that you can praise and reward him. Build this up, using whatever commands the dog knows (stay, down, come etc) until the dog is happily obeying you. Then rejoin the class, working hard to keep your dog focused; maintain a distance from the other dogs until he can ignore their presence.

USEFUL ADDRESSES AND BIBLIOGRAPHY

As you can see, it is best to start training your pup **before** you start class. All the exercises that have been discussed in this book can be taught at home and then practised in the garden, a quiet corner of the park, a friend's house, and so on. You will learn new things at club that you should then go away and practise. The trainers will show you what to do but it is up to you to continue the training at home and in your dog's everyday life.

Training clubs fulfil a variety of purposes - I use them to socialise puppies, as distractions when I am bringing a young dog along, and as a work-out for the more experienced dogs. We go to several different clubs during the week, both to instruct and train. Some hold shows and take part in rallies to help raise money for charity. There are also Kennel Club Good Citizen Dog awards which everyone can work towards. During the competitive season, we discuss how the shows went, share our successes and try to learn from our failures. At Christmas we have a brilliant party with the dogs; there is food plus fun games and competitions. For most, club is a social occasion as well as a place to learn.

I hope I have given you some ideas for training. The most important thing is to enjoy it. That way, if you make a mistake you can laugh it off and try again, with no harm done. The temptation in the beginning is to take it all too seriously and this will reflect in the dog's attitude. Don't nag the dog if things are going wrong - forget what you were doing and find something the dog *can* do so you can praise him and finish on a happy note. Then have a game with him and restore good relations. Keep him happy and he will be eager to try for you next time. If your dog enjoys being with you, you have a solid foundation on which you can build anything.

USEFUL ADDRESSES

The Kennel Club
4a Alton House Office Park
Gatehouse Way
Gatehouse Industrial Estate
Aylesbury
Bucks HP19 8XU
Tel: 0870 606 6750

Dog Training Weekly
Print House
Parc Y Shwt
Fishguard
Pembrokeshire SA65 9AP
Tel: 01348 875011
(Weekly obedience magazine who will put you in touch with your nearest club.)

BIBLIOGRAPHY

• **How to Raise a Puppy You can Live With** by *Rutherford and Neil*. ISBN 093186657X

• **Your Dog - A Guide To Solving Behaviour Problems** by *John Cree*. ISBN 1582239549

• **Your Dog - Its Development, Behaviour and Training** by *John Rogerson*. ISBN 0091734738

• **Everyone Can Train Their Own Dog** by *Angela White*. ISBN 0866225242

DOS AND DON'TS

Dos and Don'ts

Dos

• Praise your dog every time he has made an effort to obey you. Don't just issue commands, give him feedback. Also praise him for all the other good things he does, however trivial they may seem to you.

• Find out what makes your dog tick. What appeals to him? Does he go batty over balls or frisbees? Does he prefers toys to tibits? Is he easily distracted by other dogs or people? How does he react to correction? What is his concentration span? Use the answers to tune him into you, so that he finds you more fun and interesting than what is going on around him. Know his limits and don't ask for too much at once. Build it up slowly.

• Make sure the whole family use the same commands and the same techniques. Be consistent or you will confuse your dog.

• Sit down and think about what you want to achieve and how you intend to achieve it *before* you train. What you will do if things don't go right? (Plan B!)

• Wear flat shoes and clothes that won't flap in the dog's face.

• Try to start each training session with a game or ask your dog to do something easy for a titbit. Then you will both feel positive and in the right frame of mind.

• Be prepared to go back a stage or two (or even right back to the beginning) if the dog doesn't seem to understand. If he doesn't do what you ask, assume that the dog does not understand, *not* that he is being disobedient.

• Quit while you are ahead! Keep training sessions short and sweet, especially with a puppy. End on a good note, whilst the dog still wants more.

Don'ts

• Don't put yourself under pressure. It's not a race. Take your time, train with love and patience and you will get there.

• Don't train if you are not really in the mood for it (be honest with yourself!)

• Don't lose your temper if things are going wrong. Give the dog something easy to do, have a game and then call it a day.

• Don't stop practising and using the skills you have learnt. How about trying Agility, Flyball or Heelwork to Music?